Sentimental Dreams:

Inspirational Poetry of Light, Love, and Strength

Nikí R. Ferguson

Sentimental Dreams: Inspirational Poetry of Light, Love, and Strength

Published by: Blu Fountain Streams Publications LLC. Flint, Michigan 48507

Artist: Anna Ismagilova

Cover Design: Nikí R. Ferguson

Editor: FaLessia Booker, The Editing Expert. www.falessiabooker.com

Ordering Information: For quantity sales, special discounts for schools, or bulk purchases, please contact the publisher: niki_ferguson@att.net

First Edition: April 2026

ISBN: 979-8-9858174-5-4

Printed in the United States of America

Sentimental Dreams: Inspirational Poetry of Light, Love, and Strength

Dedication

To the Believer who finds the light in the darkness.
To the lover that keeps the flame aglow.
To the dreamer who hears the music in the silence.
To the encourager that creates space to breathe.
To the advocate whose voice elevates the path for the voiceless.

May your passion continue to ignite
and your purpose be loud and unapologetic.

Acknowledgements

To my family, friends, and writing community: I am thankful for your encouragement, support, and listening ear.

I thank God for His grace and creative gift.

I pray that you are all blessed by this project.

Discover more works by Nikí R. Ferguson at the end of this book.

Table of Contents

Prologue: Living Words

How do I produce words that live on the page fearlessly and without hesitation? Make them dance rhythmic beats to the tempo and leave those who hear awestruck? How do I make them shake the sound barriers and cause riots by the sheer conduct of their formation? I have reached my innermost thoughts from the depths of my core, funneling through feelings of love, joy, peace, beauty, sadness, and anger. I marvel at how words find me when emptiness resembles a bottomless pit.

Access to words is limitless, but training oneself to use them is a gift. We transform our feelings into the translations of many, empathically taking on adopted burdens. Words embrace our inner selves, where our thoughts and the world collide, where connections of neutrality become futile when our emotions are awakened.

We move words with the right meanings and descriptions to paint pictures that tell stories of diversity. Where the trajectory of our reach travels technological miles. Where our hearts cry tears stained with sadness when faced with pain and suffering. Where we reign pure delight and bliss into the loins of those hungry for satisfaction. We take pleasure in the peaceful place where our words provoke joy and happiness, connecting the universe to the unknown. They prick the heartstrings that rattle barricades. They soothe dull aches that rock us to our core.

Words are the ties that bind our dreams to reality, our desires to necessity, our complacency to actions. They live on paper to coat the air as we speak them into existence. They take on life to form a body of colorful representations of the moments of mankind and imagery of fantasy. If we are brave enough to write them and speak them, we are brave enough to become and embody them. To walk the lines where words and reality meet to tell the stories of dreams and generations matters for the ages.

Exhort

To exhort is to call the soul forward with urgency and truth, refusing to let potential remain hidden beneath fear. It is a voice of purpose that challenges one to rise.

This Too, Shall Pass

No matter how much I hype up my problem.
This, too, shall pass.
No matter how much sorrow I feel at the time.
This, too, shall pass.
No matter what trouble I go through daily.
This, too, shall pass.

I recognize God's hand on my life.
I recognize His presence has been there all the time,
I recognize His footprints in the sand.

I've looked behind me too many times,
to see the grace He's bestowed upon me.
Only to see His gifts at the end.
Only to see my answered prayers.

How did I get here?
Walking in circles.
He presented His glory
through my blinded eyes.

Yes, I say I believe.
Yes, I say I see.
Yes, I say I have laid my burdens at His feet.
I say I have faith.
But in my mind I'm saying,
"Help my unbelief."

While I'm wandering in my wilderness…
Can He trust me?
Trust me to follow through.

He said to trust Him.
To believe.
To have faith.
To speak to that mountain.
It shall be moved!

Step by step.
With the grain of a mustard seed.
I build my faith.
I am yet rebuilding my faith.

And all those things shall wash away.
While He quietly says,
"This, too, shall pass
this, too, shall pass."

How Dare You?

How dare you begin to second-guess yourself?
Don't think you are retreating to the back shelf.
You're beginning to doubt, to compare yourself.
Compared to who?
You are uniquely you.

It was I who qualified you.
I put you on display for a reason.
To showcase your gifts.
To walk into your season.
Gifts I've given you, gifts to the world.

To take as far as you can go.
It is *Me,* in whom you abide.
You can no longer hide.
Why would you?
This is not the time to conceal your light.
Shine in the darkness.
Your ray's beam is bright.

I planted that seed.
I gave you power.
Power over stinking thinking.
Power within yourself.
Power to believe.
Believe you have what it takes.
To walk on water.

I gave you vision.
I gave you wisdom.
I gave you passion.
I gave you a voice.

You are not the wallflower you pretend to be.
I gave you infinite abilities.
Ingrained in the faith of a mustard seed.
I created you to create masterpieces.

Within your humility.
Within your meekness.
Use it to your advantage.
Take control over your weaknesses.

In your discreet confidence.
Command the attention of others.
You are the quiet thunder.
Generate the lionesses' roar.
I created you to soar.

Artistic Inspiration

There is power in my stare.
As I look to the heavens,
the Lord hears my prayers.
He hears my dreams calling.
Granting the desires of my heart.

My heart brings forth light.
It emanates from my soul.
I am emboldened by my plight.
The daughter of the Most High.
Captivated in His delight.

Equipped for the fight of life.
My mind, undergirded.
The light behind my eyes
tells my story.
Elevated by His glory.

I towered above my battles.
Glowered into the face of my enemy.
Called death by his name.
Confined him to his cell.
Now victory calls my name.

Flowing from my heart
is the love I feel
from the beauty gained
overshadowing my scars.
The purpose of my healing
written in the stars.

My position is Majestic.
Bejeweled in grandeur.
Crowned with authority.
Royalty, my distinction.
Sovereignty is my Reign.

The wonder behind my gaze

amazes the bewildered soul.
Transfixed by His grace,
justified by motivation,
my purpose unfolds.

No Wasted Words

Words are thoughtful.
Words are important.
When I use them,
I am careful.

When I speak them,
I don't speak amiss.
My words are tasted before I release them into the atmosphere.
My words are never used to offend the receiver.
My words are never used for condemnation,
only reflection from a transparent place.

Written words last a lifetime.
Spoken words either sit with you for a moment,
or impact your heart to remember.

Words are precious to one's soul.
I care what others receive from my words.
Will never speak out of spite.

Prayerfully,
they come from a place of wisdom.
A place of empathy.
A place of consideration.
A place of observation.
A place of discernment.
A place of admonishment.
A place of sincerity.
A place of growth.
A place of communication.

Words give life.
Words take life.
Words harm.
Words inspire.
Words edify.
Words empower.

Extending those words
can come at a price.
Especially to those you love.
Those you admire, care about, and want to inspire.

To be better.
To listen better.
To receive better.
To look inward and examine.

I speak from a place of passion.
With passion, so people hear my heart.

But don't get it twisted.
If I didn't care, I wouldn't share.
I will not waste my words.
I *will* not waste my words
on those unwilling to hear.

To the idle reader.
if I offended you…
it was never my intent.
My intent was to find you in the ashes,
lift you into the place of insight and beauty,
and achieve perfecting purpose.

I cannot claim to be perfect,
but I have inclined my ear
to listen to wisdom,
to come from a pure place of life's resolution.
In the time of discontent, malice and personal
misunderstandings…
If my heart beats for you, it bleeds for your contentment.
I can only hope you take my sincerity to heart.

Our Trusted Guide

This is the time to trust God.
As if there has never been a time to trust Him.
How many times have you gone on autopilot?

In your own strength.
Not in His strength.
You say you trust Him
How would you know?

It's not easy.
Not easy to trust.
For so long,
doing it on your own.

Secretly wondering.
Wondering about your worthiness.
Your worthiness to ask.
Your worthiness to receive.

What if you ask amiss?
What if you asked in selfishness?
Does the mask you hide behind
keep you from moving forward?
It's time to remove it.

You need Him.
When you turned it all over,
when you said yes to Him…
He's looking for your *Yes.*
Understand the importance of God in your life.

He's working it out.
Showing Himself strong.
He's showing you His promises.
Focus your thoughts on Him.
Search for Him in the darkness.

Creator, Oh Creator.

The One who knows you.
Who knows your heart…
The doubts that overshadow your faith.
The faith that pushes over the doubt.
Your heart's intent.
Your desires.

Working on self-doubt.
Helping your unbelief.
You've been asking for His favor.
He's been showing you His favor.

One by one.
Day by day.

He's choosing you.
As you're working it out in your mind.
He's showing you the desires of your heart.
He's showing you they are possible.
Proving His faithfulness.
Are you proving your faithfulness?

You've been showing up.
Not perfectly,
but showing up.

The Lord is your helper,
in your darkest hour.
Waymaker to your heart.
He is the keeper of your dreams.

When you show up,
He listens.
Even when you think He's not there.
He is the footprint in the sand.
The ear in the heavens.
The shadow keeping watch in the darkness,
to keep away your enemy.

Choose this day whom you will serve.
Building up in His most holy faith.
His love reigns supreme.

In your quiet place,
search for Him.

Your blessings belong to Him.
He's granting each one
with miraculous favor.

Keep asking.
Keep growing.
Keep showing up.

He changes you.
Into the person you would be.
Into the person you could be.
Into the person you aspire to be.

He shows you who He is.
He shows you, even when you don't trust.
How can surrender be described?

Enter into the stillness.
Slowly remove the mask.
Reveal your transparency,
your truth.
Your desire to reveal your vulnerability,
in His presence.

Trust the Lord with your heart.
He'll help you trust yourself.
He'll help you to gain traction.
He'll help stand in His wisdom.
Lay your foundation ablaze.

Control your desire to retreat,
retreat back to chaos in the mind,

to cut and run.
He'll help you face your fears,
your doubts.

He'll help you to lean,
lean more into His heart.
Not your understanding.
but allow Him to be your guide.

I Want to Live

I want to live.
I want to live life.
I want to live life better.
Better than the lackadaisical portrayal of the daily grind.

I want to live.
Live beyond the chaos.
The chaos swirling around like a tornado,
while standing in the center
waiting to swallow you whole.

I want to live.
Not in fear of what I don't have,
but live in gratitude
for what I already possess.
With great expectation that
I will embody my true worth.

I want to live with a full heart.
Full of love even when there's pain.
I want to live past everyday anxieties.
Transform my darkest hours,
that makes it feel like stormy days.

I want to live.
Live abundantly on purpose.
Learning the significance of life's mistakes.
Finding pearls of value in the lessons they bring.

I want to live the experience of love's fullness
when recovering from its affliction.
To know the pricelessness gained
from the tear-stained windows of my soul.

Knowing that through love,
that the loves lost,
were lost to longing.
In pursuit of the one true love

that proves love's loss gets better.

I want to live life's meaning.
Knowing that I will enjoy the journey.
Knowing that burning sunrises
and amber sunsets fulfill my days.
I want to live with the change of seasons.
Expand with wisdom's reasons for being.
I want to live with the boldness
I will need to suppress the shortcomings,
that behind, I hide.

I want to live.
Live my purpose over the enemy.
Despite the enemy that wants my life to end
under circumstances, my mind and body can't comprehend.
When my soul is too tired, my spirit too fragile to defend.

I want to live.
Live a life by divine design.
That the design of my life will not be cut short by illness.
That my life will not be cut short by ill will.
that I will appreciate every morsel.

I want to live a genuine existence.
Overlooking life's complications.
Overcoming life's barriers.
Transforming with life's meaning.

I want to live with the creativity inside,
knowing that masterpieces burn within.
The value I bring resonates beyond obstacles.
That grace's pathway will be my guiding light.

Creative Light

As long as the Lord allows me to walk this earth
I have an opportunity,
a mandate to leave something positive while alive.
My legacy does not live on in birthed children,
but in words meant to give life.

I am sold out for what's right.
To inspire life through words of wisdom.
Encourage the discouraged.
Inspire the uninspired.
Break down the walls of misconceptions.

Allow my character to speak
through the eyes regarded as the minority
living among the majority.
We take hold of opportunities
we think are meant for others.

But through obedience,
walking into the assignment,
engaging with thoughtfulness
with the understanding
that tomorrow is not promised.

But it starts with me.
Pure of heart.
Sharing with one person at a time.

Captive Creative

My words sometimes fail me.
Each day is a trigger to stifle the gift of creativity.
A voice muffled by unsolicited drama.

The drama of life peering into the windows of my soul.
Struggling to break free of the chains that bind me.
Holding fast the will to lay a foundation.
A foundation of words that lay dormant on the page.

My fingers paralyzed.
Paralyzed from the exchange of my brain signals.
Malfunctioning from restriction of creativity.
My voice, struggling to find its peace.
Peace in the sea of wailing.
Wailing and complaining that covers the earth.

Searching for the sound of faith.
The sound of affirmation.
The sound of unity.
Knowing the words to say,
but seemingly becoming mute and tone deaf.

Formulating recognition.
Recognition of my former self,
to gain the traction necessary to break.
Break the barrier of stagnancy.

Waiting for my love to return with impact.
The impact of the affirming agenda.
Cognitively changing circumstances,
one word at a time.

Overlooking others obstructions.
Restricting my creativity.
Shutting out the world.
In the world lies inspiration.
In the world chaos also lies.

Finding the will to cut the ties that bind
by challenging the noise.
The noise that invades the psyche.
Finding the focus needed to change directions.
Choose uplifting words
in an imaginative way.

I want to cold-cock the clock
that challenges my time.
That steels my energy.
That weighs me down,
mentally binding me from
my words of security.

I am but one piece to the puzzle.
A puzzle of many pieces.
A puzzle of many voices,
struggling to have a say.

Enrapture

To enrapture is to capture the heart so deeply that wonder silences all else, drawing the spirit into awe. It is the gentle power of being wholly captivated.

Love's Inspiration

I cling to your love.
It provides the peace of still waters.
It gives me strength to move mountains.

Your love invigorates me
to press forward.
It conquers my fears.
It allows me to rest in your grace.

Your love motivates me to strive for more.
It empowers…

Your love allows me to dance freely in your presence.
Allows me to fly as if I had wings.
Your love challenges my restrictions.
Opens my eyes to new purpose.
Inspires me to dream beyond boundaries.

Heartbeat

My hand, placed in your hand.
My bosom connected to your masculine surface.
Our hearts rhythm in step.
Counter beats the sound I hear in unison.

Our eyes lock in yearning.
The touch I need to peer into your soul.
Those windows that reach Heaven.

My call to you, unspoken.
Your fingertip quiets my bottom lip.
Kisses, soft and lingering.

You have cocooned yourself tightly around me.
Wrapped yourself within my skin
to say you will never let go.

Our souls, intertwined within the universe.
Quietly lying as our fingers write love letters against flesh
leaving remnants of sensations along the way.

Pulses quicken as our embrace strengthens.
Your stronghold over me, captivating, yet subtle.
The flutter in my womb quickens.

The cadence of our dance pulsates through touch.
Skin to skin, breath for breath.
Mingling of love's heart beating at its core.

My essence transfers to yours.
Your pores drip into mine.
My heart pours into your cup.
Your love weaved into my DNA.

Lovestruck

Sometimes, I get caught up in how much I love you.
My life before you was preparation for the moment you stepped into my world.
My breath paused the instant you entered the room.
My stomach leapt, my heart danced.

The second our eyes met was kismet.
Our destiny began when your lips parted to speak.
Our souls interlocked, weaving fate's fabric of love.

Love's journey chose our meeting.
Center stage.
In the reflection of the moon's golden radiance.
Struck by love's brightest light.

Now that my destiny embodies you,
my identity split, encompassed by our union,
to transform my being.

Without you,
I'm drowning in quicksand.
Saved only by the branch you extended for my salvation.

Away from you,
my heart is stricken with despair.
Glowing pebbles lead back to your presence.

I remember not who I was before you.
Because of you, I am new.

Choosing Love

Loving thoughts invade my mind as I think of you.
Building with you has been a journey.
Day by day, we've lived.
We've built a foundation.
My only expectation was a hopeful life filled with love.

Growing together through tests and trials.
Thank you for choosing love.
Thank you for choosing patience.

Thank you for choosing me when you weren't looking.
Thank you for choosing unconditional in a time where some choose conditional.
Thank you for saving space for the dramatic revelations.

Thank you for daily rediscovery in the sea of the mundane.
In the seesaw of the commonplace.
In the consolation of silence.

Beckoning Lovers

I am the beauty behind all his desires.
I am the touch that sets his heart on fire.
I am the energy that propels his motivation.
I am the echo he calls to in the night.
I am the dream that takes him on his wildest journey.

I have enticed him with my stare.
Lost while looking through the windows of my soul.
My lips have softly drawn him in.

My skin trusts your touch.
My mind and body quicken with extensions of you.
I have breathed a thousand breaths to be captured by you.
Impressions of you have been etched upon my heart.
Beckoning lovers, enamored within your presence.

At Rest With You

In morning's light,
I am greeted with the snuggles of your kiss.
A welcoming acknowledgement of a new day with you.

With spring's appearance,
light shines through the windows of shuttered eyes.

Touches of newness
brush over withered wings, revitalizing nature's spirit.

I am reminded
there is tenderness in the journey.
As the years culminate, fragility enters over the generations of life.

Vulnerability increases with maturity.
Humility waters the slivers of bladed grass.

Walking through the trials of day.
Open vials of forgiveness scattered at our feet.
Old wounds evaporating under precipitating circumstances.

The daily expressions of love sprinkled through the atmosphere,
land in the ear gates of your intended
like dandelion sprays dancing in the wind.

And with the closing of night,
your embrace, with midnight kisses is comforting at rest.

Miss You

There are days when I think of the longevity of our future
How many more days will God give us on this earth together?
Contemplating the moments our bodies start to fail.
Dreading the moments our minds start to wander.
I shudder to think of the shifting tides of age,
when our activities become limited.

Yet, I reminisce about our past and our present.
The future covenant that remains
to appreciate the grace of times' ageless range.

Wrapped around each other through the night.
Those special kisses throughout the day.
The simple touches just to connect.
The piercing stares to gauge your thinking.
Those times you pull me close just to be near.
The late-night talks about the drama of our day.
The random conversations about nothing interesting at all.
When you listen without listening.
The acts of kindness done without asking.

I miss you.
I miss you in our future.

Moments

I count the moments when we're together.
Savoring the time in your presence.
The twinkling in your eyes draws me closer to you.
Your embrace feels like home.
A habitat of comfort cradled in your arms.
Resting peacefully from the day's distraction.
Each occasion I have to savor moments makes me appreciate us.
Visions of you linger in my thoughts, etched in my cerebrum.
Drawing a smile to my lips with anticipation of a soothing kiss.
Flashes of intimate moments give pause to my flesh.
With hearts aflutter, instant reflections send joy beams through my face.

Playground Fragrances

My heart catches at the touch of your lips.
The loins of my desire awaken at its pulse.
My diamond tips perk at the very thought of you.
My mountain tops heave at your sultry caress.

My body shudders.

The southern placement of your hand on my belly.
Your fingers sliding playfully in my playground.
Drunk with pleasure.
My womb constricts.

Ahh, touch me.

The uptick of my blood exalting its temperature.
Paint me with the strokes of your love.
My breathing overlaps your controlled glide.
My cup conforms around your greatness.

My cheeks flush.

I inhale your masculine fragrance.
Your aroma dances before my nostrils.
Intoxication overtakes my senses.
Adrenaline pulsating through my veins.

My mouth salivates as oils release.
My internal fibers ignite from your torch.
Burning through my layers of love.
Riding our waves of desire.

Forbidden Love

My heart throbs for you.
You were forbidden to me.

Secretly, my pining thoughts followed you.
Your smile, effervescent.
Each glance stolen at a distance.

I longed for you in my dreams.
Signals of hope plagued my mind with images of you.

I wasn't meant to have you.

You were the moment thirst first touched my lips.
I craved the taste of you.
The one who stole my heart.

My loins, weak from desire.
Heat rising in the delicate region of my core.
I have grown lovesick in your presence.

The day your vision aligned with mine.
You recognized the light behind my eyes.
The veil removed, an awareness took hold.

You made the move.
Your missing link.
The piece to your puzzle.

In that first kiss…
Our energy intertwined.
The spark quickened.

I wasn't meant to have you.

The stars positioned themselves.
Presented me, mirrored before you.
Crystalized in your mind.

I beheld your gaze.
Reflections of your stare,

pierced my heart.

Beautifully statuesque,
we stood transfixed.
Captivation befalls you.

I wasn't meant to have you.

But there, I stood.
Yours for the taking.

I'm in Love With Love

I'm in love with love.
Your essence seeps into my core.

When the ambiance is right,
the glimmer in your eyes catches the light.
The yearning in your gaze
connects my heart to yours.

Your lips bless mine at first touch.
My breath escapes.
Slow at its embrace.

Your kiss lingers on my lips.
Butterflies fluttering inside,
causing a moan's release.
My breath, apprehended.

I am caught.
Caught up in my love for you.
This dynamic that is us.

Desire arrests my being.
Loves loins leaping with longing.
My blossom blooms under your finesse.
The temperature in the atmospheric pressure, rising.

Speak to me with your body, the words you could not speak.
Your passion propels currents, capturing our desire.
Your love spills over in the strength of your acceptance.

I fell, falling deeper into the abyss of love.
Overtaken by the hand lifting me to safety.
When love rescued my heart.
When love peered into my soul.

I am in love with love.
Your touch is all I need.

Electric Fulfillment

Intertwined and locked in your embrace.
My breath mirrors your breathing in longing.
Your scintillating touch sends electric pulses through my body,
reviving the dormant impulses of my soul.
My silken tears release from the quivers of my burning desire
and the rivers of passion soak the layers of our flesh.

The thunderous roar within my loins
trembles with the girth of your storm
Every stroke of lightning
delivered beneath my surface,
causes a resurgence in my core from delivery.

I welcome your exploration of travel through my nature.
The wonder through my eyes
transfixed with yours in adoration.
You have adorned your consciousness
within my secret place,
copulating with every gesture.

Invaded my womb with the eruptions of your hunger.
Causing a reciprocal fervor of thirst,
our bodies melting from an insatiable appetite.
Our auras are fused as we indulge at our highest point of ecstasy.
The push and pull of your magnetism electrifies my inner realm.
The intensity of our heat rises within us.

Physiques glistening, droplets trickling from our skin,
activating the pheromones between us.
I am indulgently wrapped in your skin.
Reality's grasp fades.
Every gliding stroke inside my chamber
interchanged thrusts of grandeur,
transforms bursts of echoed explosions
encompassing wildly executed fulfillment.

The Encounter

He drank her in from the first time they met. They bumped into each other at a party. He excused himself as she turned to face him. She was stunning. Elegant posture. Hair swooped up in a ponytail with curls hanging at her temples. Her skin, mocha cream and flawless. Lips full and expressive. Her almond-shaped, light brown eyes glistened with bronze highlights met his also with an apology. Their worlds collided in an instant. Not able to look away from one another, he saw his life unfold in front of them. Her scent of sweet flowers mingled with his attention. This moment felt like time had stopped. He had to have her. To hold her in this instant.

Seeing this as an opportunity, he asked her to dance. She smiled and accepted. He inhaled her with his eyes. Inquiring of her name, she responded with "Dahlia." Like the flower, she was delicate with beautiful layers. He took her hand and placed his at the small of her back. She had a voluptuous hourglass figure, firm but supple. Her bosom, full. Cleavage peeking over the décolletage of her blue sheath sleeveless low-cut dress, belted at the waist. She inquired of his name, and he replied, "Rhys." *(pronounced Reese)*

She moved with grace as he led her in a slow dance. Just to be Close to You" by the Commodores was playing over the sound system. Coupled together, she was warm, as he was consumed by the aromatic heat from her bosom. Her frame fit perfectly in his arms.

She engaged him in polite conversation. Her voice was soft and velvety like a song. He thought it impossible to believe in love at first sight, but Rhys felt like he had known her all his life. There was something comforting about her. In her presence, time ceased, and he was in her moment. She invaded his psyche and was enraptured by her.

She fell quiet as he gazed into her eyes, hypnotizing her as if he were peering into her soul. It felt like he was capturing her thoughts; she felt it in her core, bewitched. His grasp felt like a safe haven. She could only rest in his embrace. He was strong and intense, but gentle as he held her. She could feel history in his arms.

He towered over her with his 6ft 4in frame to her 5ft 5in frame. Only her high heels helped close the distance between them. She drew closer to him as the dance ended. She thought he was beautiful. His fit physique produced firmly bulging biceps through his suit jacket. His white shirt unbuttoned where his tie would be. The vest underneath his jacket fit well, enhancing his chest muscles. His skin was a smooth mocha chocolate with a closely trimmed beard. His eyes were brown and glowed when the light hit just right. As he looked upon her, her insides burned with desire.

He asked if she felt like getting some air, and she agreed. She probably shouldn't be going to an isolated place with someone she'd just met, but her intuition said it was okay. There was a gazebo outside the party site, lit with romantic cascading lights all around. Emerald cushioned loveseats were placed on either side of the gazebo with gold-accented plush pillows for comfort. Trees hovered over and around the gazebo, creating an umbrella effect. The night was balmy. There was a light breeze, and the leaves rustled just slightly. The breeze rustled Dahlia's curls cascading around her face. He was taken by her glow under the amber light of the gazebo. It left him breathless to be in her presence.

Rhys pulled out her seat first and sat after she did. Taking her hand, he gazed at her before speaking. "You are beautiful," he confessed. "I have not been able to take my eyes off of you since bumping into you. It's like you appeared from nowhere, and then there was light. Forgive me if I seem over the top."

Dahlia replied with a smile, "It's okay. I wasn't sure if it was safe to feel like I've known you forever. It's awkward to say when I've just met you. There's something about you." She met his gaze with a shy confidence.

They could still hear the music playing from the speakers inside. He asked her to dance again, away from the peering eyes. He held out his hand, and she accepted. Taking her hand, they stood, and he spun her around on the gazebo floor into his arms. Their bodies close, moving in sync with each other to "If This World Were Mine," by Luther Vandross and Cheryl Lynn. The music choice of the night was old school. Her arms wrapped loosely around his waist. His arms firmly embraced the middle of her back. She nestled the side of her head into his chest. He stroked her back with his fingers lightly in an up and down motion. His fingers moved to her arms, softly sweeping her bareness. His touch sent chills down her spine. Dahlia began to melt on the inside.

Thankfully, his grasp was firm because she began to feel weak in the knees. Her hands gingerly caressed his back as she took in his scent. Inside, she was stirring, desire pulling at her core. She drew away to look up at him. Their eyes met in an inviting connection. Slowly, Rhys lowered his lips to meet hers and gently kissed her. She acquiesced with reciprocation. His lips were warm and sweet. Their kiss was slow, but all-consuming. The heat rose between them. This moment was enticing and felt like forever. The music came to an end, and though they had been lost in each other, they slowly released their grasp. Eyes piercing the other's soul. Hands still clasped together. Their connection was bound in this forever encounter.

Exalt

To exalt is to lift and honor what is worthy, speaking of it with reverence and truth. It is the act of recognizing value and boldly declaring it.

Internal Grace

My mind wants to be quiet.
Wants the saturation of peace.
Wants to be in a position of listening.
Wants the essence of my prayers to be heard.

My mind wants to withstand the quicksand of anxiety.
Wants to withstand the shaking of chaos.
Wants to embrace gratitude without unloading complaints.

My heart wants sanctification.
Over the sludge that blocks the pathways.
To the arterial impulses that navigate motivations.
Where forgiveness is the passage to salvation.

My flesh wants to be still.
My flesh covets the reception of healing and regeneration.
Detoxifying from the atmosphere of this world,
that holds the recovery of purification.

My soul wants freedom.
Freedom from its self-inflicting cell,
that holds hostage my innermost essence.
My vitality for life.

Your Presence

I am in awe of Your magnitude.
Your footprints in the sand reveal Your constant presence.
The air I inhale is a reminder of the life You breathed into me.
The exhale released is captured by the wind of Your spirit.

Your spirit breeds its essence as a lifeline of hope
into the nuances of my prayers.
Prayers delivered from the trappings of my heart
surrendering to aspirations of Your blessings.

Your name dances across my lips,
forming prayers in slumbered realms.
Consciously unconscious requests beckoning for answers.
Millions of abstract encounters waiting to be revealed,
cascading like kaleidoscopes across shaded lids.

I trust that my prayers disguised in moving dreams are safe in
Your care.
Wrapped in our covenant of faith.
Waiting for Your answers to be revealed.
Whispering in visions of unknown treasures.

Your Majesty

You pursued me like a beckoning lover
until I accepted Your offer of salvation.
You offered Your hand,
provided Your shield of safety.
Your waters of peace
stilled the thrashing tides of my consciousness.

You created an unquenchable thirst
to experience Your presence.
My mind surrenders to Your calling.
I sing praises to Your Name.
Worship at Your feet.

Basking in the tranquility of Your glory,
I celebrate the epiphany of Your revelation
in the newness of the name You created for me.
The grace You bestowed upon me.
I thank You for Your elevation.

You have reconciled me into Your embrace.
Forgiven my transgressions.
Called me into Your perfect will.
Released my conviction.
Allowed me to cast my cares.

My burdens rest on Your infinite shoulders.
Your grace captures me.
Enfolds me with Your compassion.
I find joy in Your kindheartedness,
trusting in Your goodness.
My eyes fixed on You.

I will abide under Your shadow,
covered by Your mighty protection.
Follow Your footsteps in the sand.
Align my desires with Your design for me.

Your Love for me allows me to soar.

Soar above my doubts.
Rest in the knowledge of Your abundant power.
Find divine inspiration in the manifestation of Your spirit.
Your prophetic words release my faith into action.
Keep me in Your confidence.
Exalt my belief.
Protect the source of my heart.
My lips will exhale Your Name.
My lungs will breathe Your Spirit.

I will search the world for the serenity of You.
You have given me the honor to lay at Your feet.
You allowed me to taste Your splendor.
Find myself in the magnificence of Your brilliance.
And delight in the glory of Your majesty.

Evolutions Awakening

Wrap me in the cocoon of your love.
I will rest in your warmth.
My transformation embraces your tenderness.
Your sympathetic touch soothes my heightened sensitivity.
Calms my night aches with your fingertips.
When I cry, you absorb my tears into your light,
crystallize my droplets into new hope.
You have raptured me into your heart.
Cared for me ever so delicately.
Nurtured my brokenness.
Repaired the damaged seams.
Before the bough could break.
Lifted my circumstances
into the undercurrents of billowing waves,
traveled over troubled waters.
You have protected me with your covering.
Guided me along the designated path.
I have entrusted my heart to yours.
Its condition thrives in your strength.
The vision through your eyes is radiance.
You are unchanging in your love.
Consistent with your grace.
Dedicatedly unwavering.
Slowly, you have released the veil,
initiating an uninhibited smile.
Your benevolence, satisfying.
It empowers with finesse.
My metamorphosis glistens.
Gaining new life.
Its intensity draws closer.
to evolution's awakening.
Capturing love's essence.

Seek Me With Your Whole Heart

Seek Me with your whole heart.
Seek Me in the darkness when shadows rise.
I will cast them out and bring light into your eyes.

Seek Me in the silence,
meditate on Me day and night.
When you incline your ear to My voice,
listening for the answers your soul longs to hear,
there you shall find Me.

Seek Me for the guidance you need to move through your day.
Seek Me for the wisdom to make decisions
when clarity feels out of reach.
Find Me above the highest mountains,
and in the lowest valleys.
When youthful yearnings stir your spirit
and discernment feels far from you.
Still, seek Me for the blessings your heart requires.

Seek Me in the wilderness,
when your circumstances look bleak.
Fix your eyes on Me,
and I will keep you in perfect peace.

Seek Me for understanding.
When the uncertainty feels beyond your capacity.
I hold every answer to your questions,
and the bread you require daily.
Seek Me to your heart's content.
In the quiet, mirror your heart to Mine.
Seek to please Me.
Seek to see your likeness in My image.

Seek to be fruitful,
to bear the fruit of Christ.
Where joy, kindness, and peace are your guide,
and you walk worthy in My sight.
Whatever our desires, whatever we seek…

Are we seeking Him for salvation?
To hear His voice?
To walk faithfully with Him?
Are we seeking Him…
for comfort,
for safety,
for wisdom,
for clarity and understanding,
for healing and provision?
When you seek Him, you shall find Him.

Mathew 7:7-8 says
Ask, and it shall be given to you.
Seek, and you shall find,
Knock, and it shall be opened unto you.
For everyone that asks, receives.
For everyone who seeks, finds.
For everyone who knocks,
The door shall be opened.

He is waiting.

Elevate

To elevate is to rise beyond what confines, refining the mind and spirit toward greater purpose. It is growth shaped with intention and grace.

Welcome Daylight

Welcome Daylight.
I'm thanking You for this day.
This new day that has been given.
To rise again.
To speak again.
To live again.

I'm thanking You for the will to live.
To overlook imperfections.
To fight through the uncertainties of every day.

I'm thanking You for this day.
For the activity of my limbs.
Putting one foot in front of the other.
For overcoming the pain.

I'm thanking You.
For in this day and age,
I can face my flaws
in a judgment-filled world.
Yet, still turn the other cheek.

To challenge difficult thinking.
To know myself in others
as if peering into the looking glass
where the looking glass of failure shatters.

I'm thanking You.
That the light of day shines my way
as I look over the hills
from where my help comes from.

I'm asking that light always be my guide.
That darkness is just a shadow,
and as the shadow fades,
the darkness follows.

I'm asking You that this day,

compassion grows firmly
in the depths of my soul.
And in my heart, forgiveness freely flows.

I'm thanking You this day.
The day that You have made.
Welcoming the light.
Asking to see myself in You.
To look high
instead of dwelling low.
And daily, by Your light, I am guided.

Silence

I once took you for granted.
I watched my father drive for hours on road trips in silence.
The quiet was so loud it was deafening.
Wheels, stirring on the road.
The sound, hypnotizing.
It seeped into my mind.
I was young.
I ran from silence.
It was like an uncomfortable conversation.
Maybe it was being alone with my thoughts.
Hiding behind issues and wonders that plagued my adolescence.
Filling it with noise and distractions that kept me from hearing the voice inside.

Silence.

Today, you are a treasured necessity.
Surrounded by everyday noise.
My thoughts invaded.
My mind split.
Between you and the cares of the day.

Silence.

Some days, I grasp for your embrace.
Catapulted from you by the commotion.
My eardrums, intoxicated from the pulsation of clamor.
On occasion, I'm faced with the white noise in my brain.
Containing second-guesses.
Contradicting imaginations.
Overzealous frustrations.

How can silence dance in between the noise?

In silence,
I hear…
My voice.
His voice.

My consciousness.
The echo in my prayers.
The answer to my peace.
The calm between the music.

Silence.

You are the connection to my clarity.
My conduit to transparency.
You are the doorway to my needs.

Silence.

You are my pillow.
You are the lull before my first dream.
You are the sleep before my rest.
You are my safe space.

In the silence.

The Age of Time

I think about the days I've lived.
Like daydreams, going through the motions.
Some remind me of déjà vu.
A selective moment going through this point, this time on repeat.

I think about my eyes' visual acuity.
The saturation of bustling nature bared before me.
My depth and perception with diminishing accuracy.
With dimly lit windows narrowing in around me,
I unwittingly wonder if life is beginning to shut me out.

I think about the burdens of pain.
Those captured days of unfulfilled dreams.
Of lives cut short by the enemy's enmity.
When broken egos lay down their secrets,
and sheltered skeletons reveal their shame.

I think about time's clock ticking.
Ticking with the transitions of the seasons, diminishing age.
Blessed to experience life abundantly without regret or reason.
To be blessed to see maturity's peak beyond threescore days.

I think about the nights I close my eyes to sleep.
Praying that I will wake to see another day.
That tomorrow's tomorrow will find me yet again.
When I am reminded that tomorrow is not promised.
What will I do today to carry me into eternity?

I think about when it's my time to leave this place.
Though my mind is not awake.
Will my consciousness drift through time and space
to live in a parallel Heavenly estate?

I think about the absence of my presence.
Would I linger in the minds of those I left behind?
I think about how memories of me would slowly float away.

I think about the preciousness of time to those who value it.

How wasteful to those who squander it.
How restorative to those who have almost lost it.

But mostly, think about how grateful I am for the days I've lived.
For the experiences I've had.
And praying for more days to live.

Humanity's War

We are making strides.
Strides of progression.
Strides, even in a world where we are shunned.
Where we are looked down upon.
Suspicion follows our every step.
History is a never-ending cycle that continues on,
duplicating heinous events from generation to generation.
Stigmatized from nation to nation.

When cut open, our blood flows red.
Our bodies are the same on the inside, though our outer appearances vary.
Our origins vary, but we condemn others for their differences.
Those who don't look like us,
act like us,
believe like us,
or live like us.
We vilify those who have different causes,
different cultures,
those of different nations.

We stand in the middle of wars.
Wars on gender, race, religion, and territories.

Humanity is under judgment.
We pass judgment as if there is no judge
when we should be judging ourselves.
Looking at the inward man.
Reflecting on our own imperfections, nature, and errors,
before entering into judgment of another human.
Digging up the past of those building or rebuilding for better.
We look for ways to find fault in people with whom we don't agree.
With lifestyles of people with whom we don't agree.
With ideas of people with whom we don't agree.
We become judge, jury, and executioner.

Humanity is at war!

Forgiveness is an afterthought.
Compassion is a commodity.
Empathy is relative.
Entitlement is running rampant.
The strong take from the weak.
The ill-fated are left to die.
We are stripping people of their souls to appease the power-hungry, the power seekers.

Taking from others to secure our own insecurities.
Taking from others to placate our own greed and selfishness.
Belittling others to exert control over another human being.
Rationalizing irrational behaviors from those who should know better.
Reacting to reactions not in our control.

We find ways to prey on the integrity of others.
Devalue another individual or group's worth.
Quality of life stripped, only to be taken from by force of those professing superiority.
Caught in a cycle of collateral damage from the fallout of war.

Our own personal war!
Regardless of where we stand.
There is a whirlwind of chaos in the midst of our lives.
When looking into the eyes of another,
trying to recognize the demons behind each struggle.
Wrestling with powers beyond our control.
We are in the middle of generational genocide.

Regardless of nationality, our children are dying.
Committing suicide, overwhelmed by societal pressures.
Controlled by imperial Institutions.
Demonized for mental instability.
Devastated by mental negligence.
Governmentally overhauled.
Restricted by national meddling.
Defrauded by corporate entanglements.
No matter the reason.

Killing or being killed.

We, the People, are doing our best to live.
Live in a world that belongs to us all,
while trying to belong in a world that doesn't want us.
Rejects us.
Murders us.
Because we are different.
A melting pot of beauty
that brings about fear because of our differences.
Our fallibilities, our capabilities.

But.
We are making strides.
Strides of progression
in a world that refuses to open its eyes,
to a world of people,
looking to overcome its hindering devices.
To devour bigotry, discrimination, and human annihilation,
looking for ways to push forward.

To prosper in peace.
To take over the world.

Lifted Voices

Inspired by the Black National Anthem

Our voices are many and…
We, the People, are One.
One with the multitude,
who are fighting for liberty.
Liberty: the voice of equality.

To be free in a society
where race is removed from the equation.
Where harmony is our hope,
and ***we*** can live together peacefully.
The hopes of our forefathers,
whose emboldened dreams,
manifested the civil rights by which we live.
The weight carried for our rights to justice.
So many represent the journey to freedom.
Their voices provided action for our nation
to have harmony between races.
They moved Heaven and earth for freedom's ring
so that ***we*** could stand,
hand in hand, shoulder to shoulder
without barriers that race would separate.
With the grace of Liberty.

These voices rang out for the justice of society.
They walked until Heaven and earth met
on the horizon for ***our*** freedom.
They walked with a steady beat,
even at the risk of weary feet.

They raised their voices through the storm
to overcome the silent tears of the burdened.
Of the fallen who lay bare and bled.
Speaking for the voiceless of today
to speak louder than those of yesterday.

We walk on…
Living the dream of a King.

Where the songs we ***now*** sing
ring louder than any distance.

Through ***our*** achievements, accolades, and successes,
our voices have laid foundations across boundaries throughout this nation.
Our voices have occupied rooms without defeat.
Our voices cultivated a culture woven into the fabric of civilization.
Our voices reach beyond the highest mountain.
It penetrates through the depths of the lowest valley,
lifted high above the mighty raging waters.
Our voices are heard throughout nations.
Traveled through generations
when ***our*** predecessors travailed to get us here.
When the conversation is still about the rights of ***our*** Freedom
Where ***we***, the voice of ***this*** generation
covers the past and saturates our future.

Where ***our*** eyes are lifted to the skyline.
Where ***our*** light gives life to our fight.
Where ***our*** voices ring louder than the chaos.
Where Liberty shines her light in the darkness.
We rise against hateful rhetoric.

Liberty does not care about ethnicity.
She cultivates unity.
She encourages ***our*** voices to sing out in harmony.
Striving with ***one voice.***
Reaching Heaven's gates.
Will ***our*** unconsciousness be what divides us?
Or ***will*** consciousness ***be*** what binds us?
Let ***us*** be mindful of the legacy from which ***we've*** come.
Look ahead to the legacy of strength that ***we*** will leave.
Our collective voices can calm the thunderous seas.

I Exist

I exist in a world where darkness meets the light. Where good and bad are subjective, depending on your perspective. I exist in a world where joy belongs to everyone, but only a few find the joy they are truly meant to have, or where joy is overshadowed by pain.

I exist in a world where my Creator wanted all to experience His love, yet some are subjected to selective worth. As if we get to choose who God blesses and who He doesn't. I exist in a world where society covets the value of the dollar but not the value of the soul. Where humanity doesn't have a face unless pockets run deep. Where good and bad have a price tag. Whether the rich or poor are determined by the color of your skin or the zip code in which you live. I exist in a world where negativity and insult are the pride of life, regardless of the heritage of perseverance and self-worth. Where assumptions made based on personal preference or bias are prevalent, where sacrifice and hard work are overlooked. I exist in a world where my life expectancy may be determined by the prejudices of cultural misconceptions. I exist in a world where the legacy of my ancestors has been demolished by attempted erasure. Where the amputation of my existence and the value of my ancestors accomplishments is a constant debate. I exist in a world where children are under attack emotionally, physically, and spiritually from subliminal stimulation and explicit communication. I exist in a world where judgment outweighs discernment, and compassion is overlooked with indifference.

I exist in a world where my existence was written in the stars, and the earth holds space for my steps. The world is greater than my existence, yet space was made for me to coexist. To be present, to take steps beyond its inhabitants before, with, and who have yet to come.

The state of my existence doesn't determine the condition of my wealth or lack thereof but determines the condition of my heart and the ability to be grounded and be planted firmly where I stand. To ensure the pebbles I leave behind are a guide to where I've been.

Somebody

I am somebody's somebody.
Yet, I have been slain.
Taken back into the earth
from which I came.
Your disdain for me is evident
in the lashing of your tongue.
Against me, you came.

I am somebody's somebody.
Yet, my life is worthless to you.
In selfishness, you see no life.
Anger prevails, if only to avenge your name.
To my grave, you have sent me
with the hatred you have for me.

I am somebody's somebody.
But my life was snatched.
Snatched from a disagreement, a stare, an action,
my skin color, reactions.
All because you have a weapon.

I am somebody's somebody.
Yet, you dismembered a life.
One you couldn't control
because of greed, bigotry, or even misunderstanding.
My life means nothing to you
when your schemes reek of selfish propaganda.

My life may mean nothing to you.
You have taken me from my family.
Those of whom I matter to.
But consider the mirror.
What if it were you?
Aren't you somebody's somebody?
Will there be compassion for you?

If This is Love

If love is understanding and does not judge,
I hope that you will give me grace when I'm not perfect,
and fall short of your expectations.

It would seem you hold me in higher esteem
because you are perfect and rarely make mistakes.

If love is respectful and cares for my well-being,
I hope that it will grant me respect when we disagree.
We are not always right, but it appears you can never be wrong.

If love is gentle, sweet, and tender,
I hope that it will replace the harshness with kindness and
patience.
Since it is always expected in return.

I don't want your love to be my liability.
Agape loves despite my faults.

It opens the doors to forgiveness.
Love is the keeper of God's grace.
The deliverer of His mercy.

Love does not fail to exhort.
It grants trust and warrants favor.
It does not despise.
It is just because.

Love is charitable.
It should be regardless of what I can do for you.
Love is not conditional to your expectations.
I may fall short, a distance from a pedestal.

Is contempt a condition of your love?

And He Created Woman

At my creation, I was called woman.
Female, feminine.
A natural nurturer.
The DNA of my Father.
The original Creator.

I am fearfully and wonderfully made.
Made in the image of my creator.
Formed from the clay of the potter.
Taken from the rib of man.
Half to make a whole.

My body, created to receive seed.
My body, created to conceive and to carry life.
To birth generations through my loins.

My hips widened to adjust to the life growing inside.
My womb quickens with seeds of evolution.
My bosom supple, brims with nutrients.
My body travails to bring forth life.

My body was created with purpose.
My body cannot be duplicated.
It cannot be counterfeited or mimicked for authenticity.

My genetics are woven into the fabric of my DNA.
My blueprint registers my name.
My Creator Divine formulated my creation.

He spoke my beginning.
He will receive my ending.
I will return to Him the way He created me.

Flesh of His flesh.
His original masterpiece.
The genesis of my feminine individuality.

Epilogue

Love Letter to Poetry

You found me by happenstance. You were a thought that foreshadowed my world. Each line lay a foundation of what was to come. You spoke to me in soft tones. Eloquent words moved me to emotion, allowing your whispers to open the floodgates of penned soliloquies that melted hearts.

You commanded my attention, speaking to me with your lyrical rhyme. Romancing my heart with melodic harmonies. My mind's rationality opened to new expressions. The beauty of your cadence fell from the pages. Your voluptuous words danced between my fingertips, creating whimsical verses flowing fluidly from my lips.

You held my affection, building upon your story to write ballads of love. Massaging my consciousness above my subconscious, allowing me to dream visions of intimacy from the colors of your artistry. You have painted your strokes like calligraphy engraved onto the parchment of my soul. Constructed stanzas only to escape from my lips to reveal your exquisite nature. Your unbridled beauty lay at my feet.

My imagination flourished, bewitched by your secrets. Unveiling your love in abundance through humility in verse, penetrating me to my core. Adoration befell me and tempted me beyond reason. Your decadence rich, my ears opened to receive and reveal your sonnets. I long for our continuous affair. Your balladry causes my knees to swoon. I sway from your song composed to entice me. I hear the harpist's strings billowing her notes as you engage me with your Shakespearean flow.

You have tainted my lips with serendipitous accounts of pleasure for the words you evoked from my being. Entangled me in the foundation of your compilations. Your words have transfused my emotions with your pillow talk. Sent me through merry-go-rounds of desire and angst. Consoled my moods from your laced, formulated words, dripping with seduction.

My soul speaks from the place of new birth, at the longing of your enticement. My illumination delights in your presence. You have begun a realm of pleasure in the lyrics you exhaled while breathing into me. I shall breathe you in as air and release you out as life onto the pages of divine inspiration. Cultivating the beauty behind the voice of the free-flowing liquid stains. Your poetic frames spilled over on the lines you inhabit. My thoughts converge with translating heartfelt languages that enlighten one's soul.

How do I love thee? Let me count the ways.
You have inspired my admiration, my love, my devotion to the inhabitation of your language.

Sincerely,
Lover of Poetry
Simply Nikí Ferguson

Also by Nikí R. Ferguson

Spiritual Thoughts, Intimate Expressions: An Inspirational and Reflective Book of Poetry

Images of Me: Poetry and Reflective Compositions

Illuminated Soul: A Collection of Poetic Reflections

Rose Petals and Embers: Poetic Short Stories for Lovers

www.ingramcontent.com/pod-product-compliance
Lightning Source LLC
LaVergne TN
LVHW020658100826
845148LV00012B/2545
* 9 7 9 8 9 8 5 8 1 7 4 5 4 *